Miriam and Moses

Exodus 1:1–2:10

Egypt was filled with the Children of Israel. Pharaoh made all of them slaves.

But this was not enough for Pharaoh. "In a war they might join our enemies and fight against us," he said.

Pharaoh ordered two Hebrew midwives to kill all the baby Israelite boys as they were born. But the women let the babies live. So Pharaoh turned to his own people. "Throw them into the river!" he commanded the Egyptians.

One mother had a plan to save her son. She smeared sticky tar all over a basket so it would not leak. Then she put her baby in the basket, and hid it among the reeds near the shore of the river.

"Watch the basket," she told her daughter, Miriam. So Miriam watched. Miriam saw Pharaoh's daughter come to bathe in the river. She watched the princess discover the basket.

"This must be a Hebrew baby!" the princess cried when she opened the basket. And she took pity on the crying baby.

Miriam came forward out of the reeds. "I know a woman who can nurse the baby," Miriam told the princess. And she brought the baby's own mother to care for him.

When the boy grew, the princess made him her son, and named him Moses. "For I pulled him out of the water," she said. And so Moses, the Hebrew baby, became the son of an Egyptian princess.

My D'var Torah

Moses and Pharaoh

Exodus 3–14

Moses left Egypt, but God told him to go back. "Go tell Pharaoh to let my people go."

So Moses went back to Egypt. "The God of Israel commands 'Let my people go,'" he said to Pharaoh.

"NO!" said Pharaoh.

God sent plagues that tormented the Egyptians. After each plague Moses said, "Let my people go."

"NO!" said Pharaoh.

Finally God sent a plague that killed the first-born son of every Egyptian family. Not a single house lay untouched by death. A loud cry went up in Egypt, and Pharaoh called for Moses.

"Take the people and GO!" cried Pharaoh.

The Israelites rushed to leave Egypt. They grabbed up their unbaked bread before the dough even had time to rise, and followed Moses.

But Pharaoh changed his mind. His army chased the Israelites to the Sea of Reeds. The Israelites were terrified. "It was better for us to be slaves in Egypt than to die in the wilderness!" they cried.

"See what God will do," said Moses.

Moses stretched his hand out over the water. It split apart and the Israelites crossed to the other side.

The Egyptians tried to follow. The water came crashing down and swept Pharaoh's army away.

When the Israelites saw the powers God had used to save them from Egypt, they trusted in God, and in their leader, Moses.

My D'var Torah

The Israelites and God's Laws

Exodus 19–24

At Mount Sinai God said to Moses, "Tell the people: If you will hear My voice and obey My laws, you will be My treasured people."

And the people said, "All that God has spoken, we will do." Then they washed their clothes, made themselves ready, and waited at the foot of the mountain.

On the third morning, the mountain was covered in clouds. Lightning flashed and thunder crashed and a blast from the shofar made the people tremble. And God came down in fire and smoke, and spoke to the Children of Israel the words of the Ten Commandments:

1. I am the One God. You shall have no others.
2. Do not make idols to pray to in My place.
3. Do not speak falsely in My name.
4. Remember Shabbat, and keep it holy.
5. Honor your father and your mother.
6. Do not murder.
7. Do not be false to your wife or husband.
8. Do not steal.
9. Do not lie about your neighbor.
10. Do not wish for your neighbor's belongings.

My D'var Torah

And the people promised to be faithful and to serve God. "All that God has spoken, we will do," they said.

God called to Moses. "Come. I have written all the laws on tablets of stone so that you can teach the people." And Moses went up the mountain to receive the tablets with God's laws.

Ruth and Naomi

Ruth 1–4

After her husband and her sons died in Moab, Naomi decided to return home to the Land of Israel.

"Go back to your families," Naomi said to her sons' wives. One agreed, but the other refused to leave Naomi. Her name was Ruth.

"Where you go, I will go," Ruth said to Naomi. "Your people will be my people. Your God will be my God." And she followed Naomi back to the Land of Israel.

The two women had very little food. But it was the harvest season. "I will go into the fields," said Ruth. "I will walk behind the workers and pick up grain they leave behind."

A farmer named Boaz owned the field Ruth chose. Boaz knew that Ruth and Naomi were alone and hungry. "Return only to my field," Boaz said to Ruth. Then he told his workers to leave extra grain behind for her to find. And Ruth shared all this with Naomi.

Boaz saw that Ruth was kind. He saw that she was loyal to Naomi.

"You are a fine woman," Boaz said to Ruth. "I will marry Ruth," he said to Naomi.

My D'var Torah

God blessed Ruth and Boaz. They had a son named Obed. And Obed's son was Jesse. And Jesse's son was David. And David grew up to become King of Israel. This was the blessing God gave to Ruth for being loyal to Naomi and to God, and choosing the faith of the Jews.

David and Goliath

I Samuel 17

Israel was at war. The enemy had a secret weapon. It was a giant named Goliath.

"Who will fight against me?" roared Goliath. No one wanted to fight a giant. Everyone was afraid. But a boy named David was not afraid.

David's brothers were soldiers. David was a shepherd. He kept wild animals away from his father's sheep. Sometimes he killed them with his slingshot.

One day David took food to his brothers. He saw Goliath. He heard Goliath's booming voice. He saw that the soldiers were afraid to fight the giant.

David was not afraid. "God helped me kill a lion and a bear," he said. "With God's help I know I can kill a giant." David took his shepherd's stick. He took his slingshot. He took a bag filled with smooth stones. And he set out to fight Goliath.

Goliath laughed when he saw David. "Do you think you can stop me with a stick?" he roared.

"I will stop you with God's help," said David.

David took a stone from his bag and put it in his slingshot. Carefully he aimed. Then sent the stone flying. It hit Goliath right in the middle of his forehead. The giant fell to the ground.

David had killed Goliath. The war was over. The Israelites had won. And this small, brave boy would someday become king of Israel.

My D'var Torah

Solomon

I Kings 3

Solomon, Israel's third king, did not dream of riches, or long life, or death for his enemies.

King Solomon's dream was to take care of the people of Israel with wisdom.

One day, two women came before King Solomon. "We live in the same house," said the first woman. "I had a baby. Three days later, she had a baby. But her baby died. That night I saw her take my baby and put the dead one in its place. Make her give my baby back!"

"No!" said the second woman. "The live baby is my son! The dead one is yours."

"Bring a sword!" ordered King Solomon. "I will cut this baby in two. Each of you will get half. That will be fair."

"I agree," said the second woman. "Then the baby will be neither hers nor mine."

But the first woman began to cry. "No! Please! No!" she begged. "Give the baby to her, then. Just please don't hurt him."

King Solomon now knew the truth. "You would rather give your son away than let him be hurt," he said to the crying woman. "I know you are his real mother." And King Solomon let the crying woman keep her baby.

Solomon ruled in Israel for many years. His decisions were just and wise. The people loved him. They helped him build the Holy Temple in Jerusalem. And even today, they tell stories about Solomon, the wise king of Israel.

My D'var Torah

Fit for a King

Esther wants to make a fabulous feast for the king so he will grant her wish. Help her by drawing some favorite foods to complete her banquet.

How do YOU feel when someone makes your favorite food for you?

Loyalty to the Jewish People

How did Esther show her loyalty to the Jewish people?

Esther did not stand by and let Haman hurt the Jews. Esther made the king feel happy, and then told him her secret. She told the king she was a Jew, too. She made the king care about her people. She saved them from the evil Haman.

How can you show loyalty to the Jewish people?

Color Me Loyal

There are many ways to be loyal to the Jewish people. Choose one below and color the picture. How did you decide?

Light Shabbat candles

Attend synagogue

Give tzedakah

What holiday celebrates Queen Esther and her loyalty to the Jewish people?

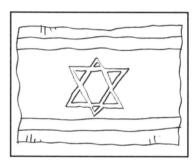

Visit Israel

Ask at Home

What story does someone in your family tell about showing loyalty to the Jewish people?

4

Copyright © 2008 Behrman House, Inc., Springfield, NJ, www.behrmanhouse.com; Author and Project Manager: Vicki L. Weber; Design: Stacey May; Story Illustration: Giovannina Colalillo; Activity Illustration: Bot Roda; Photo: David Turnley/Corbis; Printed in China; ISBN-10: 0-87441-826-7; ISBN-13: 978-0-87441-826-2

Rescue at Sea Word Search

Find and (circle) the words shown in the word bank. Copy the **red** letters onto the spaces below to see who was trying to hide.

Word Bank

BOAT	STORM		FISH
SAIL	WIND	RUN	SEA

F	I	S	H	J
W	O	T	M	P
I	B	O	A	T
N	S	R	U	N
D	E	M	A	L
S	A	I	L	H

___ ___ ___ ___ ___

Caring about Others

Jonah's words saved the city of Nineveh. Why was he angry that God did not destroy it?

Jonah told the people of Nineveh they would be destroyed for their evil ways. His words helped them change their ways. But Jonah was angry that his prediction did not come true. He cared more about being right than about saving the people of Nineveh.

When someone makes a mistake, what is more important, punishment or forgiveness? Why?

3

Show You Care

When we care about others, we try to help them. Circle an object in each picture that can keep each person safe. What do you think each person is saying?

Ask at Home

Jonah did not want to be a prophet. What helps you do a job you might not want to do?

Copyright © 2008 Behrman House, Inc., Springfield, NJ, www.behrmanhouse.com; Author and Project Manager: Vicki L. Weber; Design: Stacey May; Story Illustration: Giovannina Colalillo; Activity Illustration: Bot Roda; Photo: Corbis; Printed in China; ISBN-10: 0-87441-826-7; ISBN-13: 978-0-87441-826-2

Jonah

Jonah 1–4

God called Jonah to be a prophet. "Go to Nineveh," God said. "Tell the people I will destroy the city for their evil ways."

But Jonah did not want to be a prophet. So he ran away. He took a boat to sail far from God.

God sent a storm to follow the boat. The wind blew and waves crashed all around it. The sailors on the boat were terrified.

"Throw me overboard," said Jonah. "The fault is mine." So the sailors threw Jonah into the sea.

A huge fish swallowed Jonah. For three days Jonah was trapped inside. Jonah prayed to God, and the fish spit him out onto dry land.

"Now go to Nineveh!" God said to Jonah. This time, Jonah went.

"In forty days God will destroy this city!" Jonah shouted as he walked through the streets of Nineveh. The people heard Jonah and believed his words. They turned from their evil ways, and asked God for mercy.

And so God did not destroy Nineveh after all.

Jonah's prediction had not come true. This made him angry. "I would rather die than live," he said.

"Are you angry because I did not punish the people of Nineveh?" God asked. "Should I not care about people who are trying to learn right from wrong?"

My D'var Torah

Esther

Esther 1–7

sther had a secret.

The king had chosen Esther to be his queen. He knew he loved her. He knew that Esther and her cousin Mordechai had stopped an evil plot to kill him. But the king did not know Esther's secret. He did not know that she was a Jew.

Haman was the king's advisor. The people of the city had to bow before him. But Mordechai would bow only before God. This filled the proud Haman with rage.

"The Jews refuse to obey your laws," Haman said to the king. "If it please Your Majesty, I will choose a day to execute them all."

The Jews of the city were terrified. "You must speak to the king!" Mordechai begged Esther. "Even your own life will be in danger."

Esther made feasts to honor the king. This made him very happy. "Whatever you wish will be yours," he said.

"I wish for my life," said Esther. "I wish for Mordechai's life, and the lives of my people. There is a man who plans to destroy us all."

"Who dares?" said the King. "You are my queen. Mordechai saved my life!"

My D'var Torah

"We are also Jews," said Esther, "And Haman plans to kill us all."

"Then let Haman be the one to die!" ordered the king.

And so each year Jews tell the story of how Queen Esther revealed her secret and saved the Jewish people.

Whose Baby?

Help King Solomon return the baby to its real mother.

Seeking Wisdom

What made Solomon a great king?

Solomon did not ask for money. He did not want God to kill his enemies for him. Solomon wanted to be able to help his people. He wanted wisdom.

Think of someone you know who is wise. How can you tell?

Write the letter W under the pictures that show someone seeking wisdom.

Ask at Home

Where would you look for wisdom?

Copyright © 2008 Behrman House, Inc.., Springfield, NJ. www.behrmanhouse.com; Author and Project Manager: Vicki L. Weber; Design: Stacey May; Story Illustration: Giovannina Colalillo; Activity Illustration: Bot Roda; Photo: Randy Faris/Corbis; Printed in China; ISBN-IO: 0-87441-826-7; ISBN-13: 978-0-87441-826-2.

A Giant Fight

Circle three things David took with him to fight Goliath.

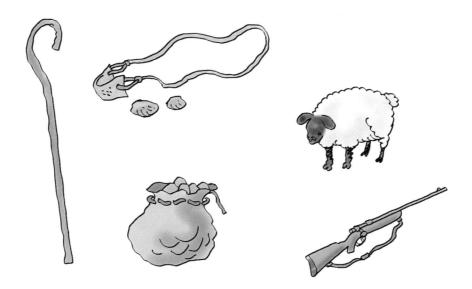

David also took something no one could see. Do you know what it was?

Being Brave

What made David brave?

Our tradition tells us that David felt God helping him protect his father's sheep from wild animals. David said he was not afraid of Goliath because he knew God would help him fight the giant too.

What helps you be brave?

We sometimes need to do things that make us feel afraid, like getting a shot, or going to the dentist. We have to find a way to be brave. Draw yourself being brave.

I am brave when I _____ .

Ask at Home

Who is the bravest person you know? Why?

Copyright © 2008 Behrman House, Inc., Springfield, NJ, www.behrmanhouse.com; Author and Project Manager: Vicki L. Weber; Design: Stacey May; Story Illustration: Giovannina Colalillo; Activity Illustration: Bot Roda; Photo: Charles Gulung/zefa/Corbis; Printed in China; ISBN-10: 0-87441-826-7; ISBN-13: 978-0-87441-826-2.

Help Ruth Find Food

Connect the dots to help Ruth gather enough food for herself and Naomi.

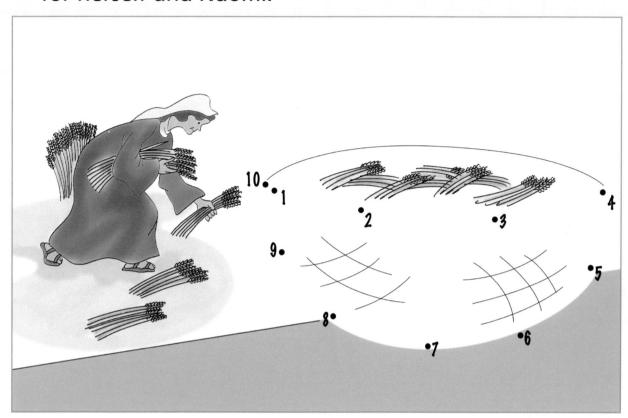

Feeding the Hungry

Why did Boaz leave grain in his fields?

It was the custom in ancient Israel for farmers to let poor people pick up fallen grain from the fields at harvest time. Picking up the fallen stalks was called gleaning. By leaving extra grain behind, Boaz helped Ruth gather enough food for herself and Naomi.

Today hungry people in our country cannot find food in a field. How can we help them?

The Helping Path

Draw a line from each child on the left to the object on the tzedakah box that he or she needs.

Ask at Home

Ruth was not a Jew, but decided to follow Jewish ways. Do you know someone like Ruth?

Copyright © 2008 Behrman House, Inc., Springfield, NJ, www.behrmanhouse.com; Author and Project Manager: Vicki L. Weber; Design: Stacey May; Story Illustration: Giovannina Colalillo; Activity Illustration: Bot Roda; Photo: Richard Lobell; Printed in China; ISBN-10: 0-87441-826-7; ISBN-13: 978-0-87441-826-2.

Message at Sinai

Find and (circle) the words in the word bank below.

MOSES   SINAI   ISRAEL   OBEY   GOD

```
O  B  E  Y  I  A
M  T  G  H  E  O
N  M  O  S  E  S
O  G  D  N  E  O
D  S  I  N  A  I
I  S  R  A  E  L
```

Copy the red letters onto the lines below to find God's special message to the Children of Israel.

___ ____ _____ _____ _____.

Serving God

What does it mean to serve God?

The Torah tells us that the Israelites promised to serve God by remembering God's laws, and following them. "All that God has spoken, we will do," they said.

What will you do this week to serve God?

Circle the pictures that show people remembering to serve God. Draw a <u>line</u> under the person who has forgotten to serve God.

Ask at Home

What is a good way to honor a parent?

Copyright © 2008 Behrman House, Inc., Springfield, NJ, www.behrmanhouse.com; Author and Project Manager: Vicki L. Weber; Design: Stacey May; Story Illustration: Giovannina Colalillo; Activity Illustration: Bot Roda; Photo: moodboard/Corbis; Printed in China; ISBN-10: 0-87441-826-7; ISBN-13: 978-0-87441-826-2.

Let My People Go!

Help Moses lead the Israelites out of Egypt.

BONUS! Find and (circle) two plagues God sent to torment the Egyptians.

Trusting in God

Why did the Israelites need to learn to trust in God?

The Israelites had been slaves all their lives. They did not know what it was to be free. They needed trust in God to keep going, and to walk across the Sea of Reeds even though they were afraid.

How can thinking about God help you do something difficult?

I Think I Can!

It can be hard to try something new, like riding a bike the first time or learning to swim. Draw yourself trying something new.

Ask at Home

Do you remember your first day of school? What made you nervous? What made you feel better?

Save Moses

Circle the people who helped save baby Moses.

Protecting Life

Who really saved baby Moses?

It took many people to save baby Moses. The Hebrew midwives refused to follow Pharaoh's orders. Moses' mother hid him in a basket by the river. Miriam watched over the baby. Pharaoh's own daughter drew the baby from the water to keep as her own.

Name someone you know who protects life.

It's A Match!

Draw a line from each person who helps protect life to the tool he or she needs to do the job.

How can you protect life with a tzedakah box?

 ## Ask at Home

What can you do to help protect your own life?

4

Copyright © 2008 Behrman House, Inc., Springfield, NJ; www.behrmanhouse.com; Author and Project Manager: Vicki L. Weber; Design: Stacey May; Story Illustration: Giovannina Colalillo; Activity Illustration: Bot Roda; Photo: Ned Frisk Photography/BrandX/Corbis; Printed in China; ISBN-10: 0-87441-826-7; ISBN-13: 978-0-87441-826-2.